TREASURE HUNTING

BY
Ian Elliott Shircore

ILLUSTRATED BY
Ed Carr

MACDONALD

Adapted and published
in the United States
by Silver Burdett Company,
Morristown, N.J.
1980 Printing

ISBN 0-382-06459-3
Library of Congress
Catalog Card No. 80-52199

About this book

This book has been carefully planned to help you become an expert. Look for the special pages to find the information you need. **RECOGNITION** pages, with a **red flash** in the top right-hand corner, contain all the essential information to know and remember. **PROJECT** pages, with a **grey border,** suggest some interesting ideas for things to do and make. At the end of the book there is a useful **REFERENCE** section.

Looking for treasure

Everybody has found treasure of some sort or another. You are bound to have found an old coin, badge or piece of jewellery when digging in the garden, walking along a country footpath or playing on the beach. But it doesn't happen very often. And a single coin, unless it is very rare or very old indeed, cannot really be called treasure.

In spite of the stories about pirate gold and Pieces of Eight, buried in huge chests on faraway desert islands, there is real treasure that you can find in the area where you live. It is there because people have hidden it underground, thrown it away as rubbish or simply lost it.

If you know where to look, how to look and the sort of things to look for, you are sure to find treasure. This book will tell you how to go about it.

Treasures from the past

Every year or two, each country in the world produces hundreds of thousands of new coins. This is not because the old coinage has worn out. It is because millions of perfectly good coins disappear every year. People lose purses. They drop money when they are on the beach or having a picnic in the country or counting their change after coming out of a shop. Their parents and grandparents and ancestors for many generations have all lost money and other objects in much the same ways.

Beautiful coloured bottles, potlids and clay pipes lie buried where they were thrown away on Victorian rubbish dumps. With a few tools and a little knowledge about where to look, you can begin to find these treasures from the past.

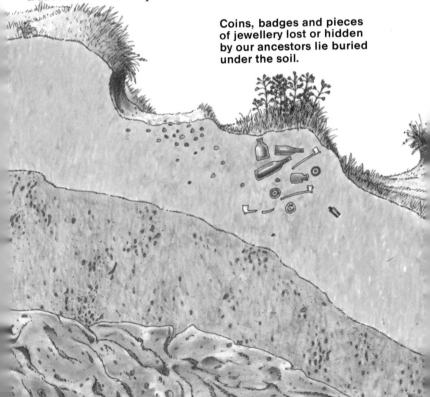

Coins, badges and pieces of jewellery lost or hidden by our ancestors lie buried under the soil.

Different kinds of treasure

Knowing what is junk and what is interesting or valuable is as important as knowing where to look for treasure. Silver coins may be so tarnished that you won't realise what you've found until you have had a chance to look at them closely. Unusual bottles may look quite ordinary until you clean them up. When in doubt, take home everything you find and make up your mind later about what to keep for your collection.

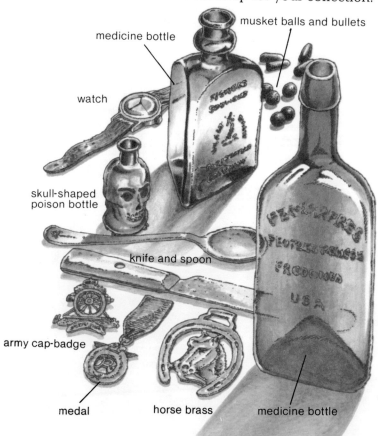

medicine bottle

musket balls and bullets

watch

skull-shaped poison bottle

knife and spoon

army cap-badge

medal

horse brass

medicine bottle

sword

stoneware
mustard pots

14th-century
silver axe head

shoe buckle

ginger beer bottle

clay pipes

keys and rings

necklace

coins, old and modern

potlid

'postbox' ink bottle

spearhead

arrowhead

Starting off

Search in your living room.

Part of the secret of successful treasure hunting is knowing how to search. But it is even more important to know the sort of places where things are lost or hidden. Try to put yourself in the shoes of someone two or three centuries ago. Ask yourself how he would have lived, worked and spent his free time. People haven't changed that much over the years. The sunny corner of the garden where your family enjoys sitting today was just as sunny, and probably just as popular, a hundred years ago.

Beginner's luck

This sort of detective work is what makes a successful treasure hunter. So why not start by thinking of places to search at home? Sit in an armchair and feel down the sides of the seat cushion. You are almost certain to find a couple of modern coins.

Skirting boards

Now look around you. You will probably see a small crack at the bottom of each wall where the skirting board meets the floor.

Coins are often knocked into these cracks when the floor is swept. Wall-to-wall carpets were rare until about 20 years ago and vacuum cleaners only date back to 1901, so older houses often hold surprising numbers of these forgotten coins. Slide the end of a plastic ruler along the crack and you will be able to fish them out.

Lofts and sheds

Your attic or garden shed may be full of things that you think are just bits of junk. But many people collect old comics and newspapers, model cars and toy soldiers, picture frames and cigarette-card albums and these can all be worth quite a lot of money today.

Ask your parents if you can rummage through the things in the loft — you may find 'junk' that you can sell to an antique dealer. Why not save the money you make from this until you have enough to buy yourself a metal detector?

Climb up and look in the loft.

The equipment you will need

Treasure hunting need not be an expensive hobby at all. At times you will need to wear the tough, warm clothing shown on this page.

Most of the other equipment, like trowels, sieves and spades, can usually be borrowed rather than bought.

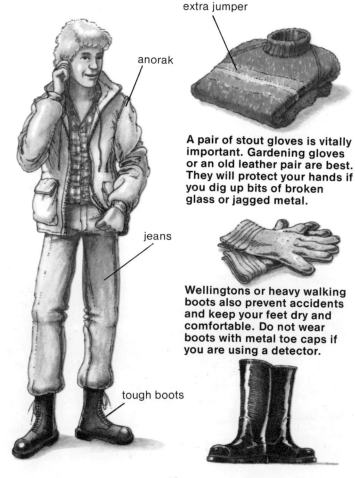

extra jumper

anorak

jeans

tough boots

A pair of stout gloves is vitally important. Gardening gloves or an old leather pair are best. They will protect your hands if you dig up bits of broken glass or jagged metal.

Wellingtons or heavy walking boots also prevent accidents and keep your feet dry and comfortable. Do not wear boots with metal toe caps if you are using a detector.

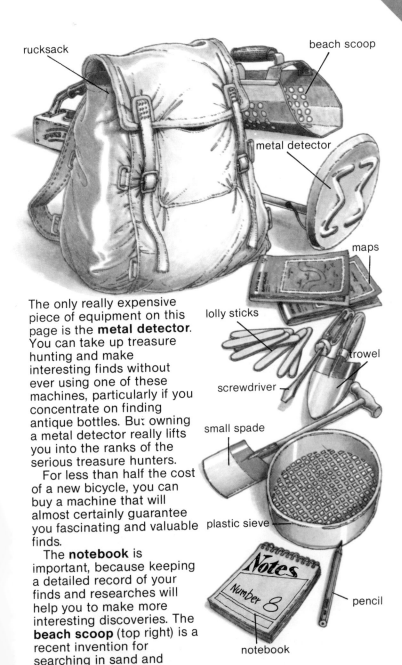

rucksack

beach scoop

metal detector

maps

lolly sticks

trowel

screwdriver

small spade

plastic sieve

Notes

Number 8

pencil

notebook

The only really expensive piece of equipment on this page is the **metal detector**. You can take up treasure hunting and make interesting finds without ever using one of these machines, particularly if you concentrate on finding antique bottles. But owning a metal detector really lifts you into the ranks of the serious treasure hunters.

For less than half the cost of a new bicycle, you can buy a machine that will almost certainly guarantee you fascinating and valuable finds.

The **notebook** is important, because keeping a detailed record of your finds and researches will help you to make more interesting discoveries. The **beach scoop** (top right) is a recent invention for searching in sand and gravel.

Metal detectors

A metal detector is like a time machine that lets you see into the past. Even the cheapest, simplest models, costing less than £20, will open up a whole new world for you to explore.

With a metal detector, you can 'scan' the top few centimetres of the soil and find the coins, badges, tools and musket balls which have been buried there for years. Until the detector was invented a few years ago, these objects might just as well have vanished for ever — even though they lie just below the surface of the earth.

The 'BFO' metal detector

The simplest type of metal detector is called a 'BFO' (beat frequency oscillator). When it is switched on and tuned in, it gives out a humming sound as it is swept over the ground at a height of two or three centimetres.

If it detects a piece of metal, the humming note changes quite sharply so that the operator can pinpoint the 'target' and dig it up.

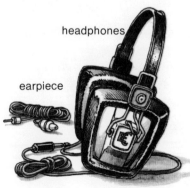

headphones

earpiece

Most detectors have loudspeakers. They are helpful when you are working as part of a team, as everyone can hear when a target has been found.

But the noise can be very irritating after a while and can sometimes be drowned out by the noise of traffic, aircraft or the waves on the seashore. Professional searchers usually prefer to use headphones or an earpiece.

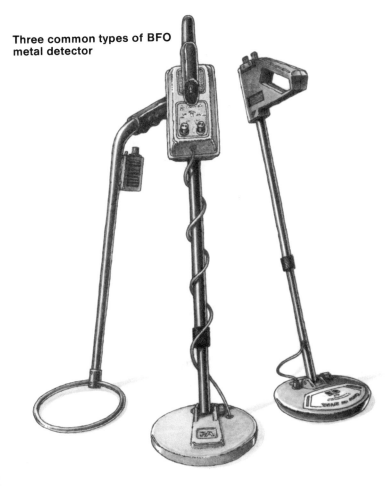

Three common types of BFO metal detector

BFOs can be very good all-purpose machines, especially for children, who have much more sensitive hearing than older people. They are not quite as simple to use as the more expensive 'IB' (induction balance) machines, but they definitely reward the hunter who puts in a lot of practice with them.

One of the most famous recent treasure hoards, consisting of nearly 100 gold sovereigns and guineas, was found by two schoolboys who were using a cheap BFO. (See page 45.)

How a metal detector works

All metal detectors work on the same scientific principles. The **search coil** acts as a **magnet**, when **electricity** from the battery is passed through it. If the search head is brought near a metal object, a current of electricity is set up in the target and the search head is then able to detect it.

In a simple BFO machine, there are two **oscillators**. These are electrical devices that 'hum' at a pitch far too high for the ear to hear.

One of them stays at a fixed pitch, but the other is tuned to a slightly higher rate of 'hum'. The machine mixes the two 'hums' together and this makes a much lower signal, a real humming noise that you can hear through the speaker. When you find a target, the electricity generated in the metal object changes the 'hum' of the higher oscillator. This causes the real hum that you hear to change to a higher note too. More expensive detectors have even more complicated circuits, but they still work by picking up the current generated in the metal target.

The search head of a BFO machine

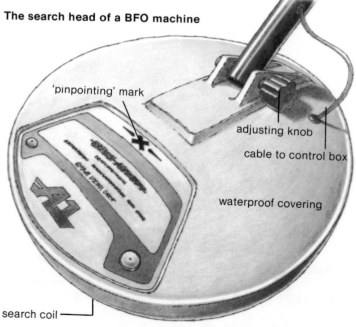

'pinpointing' mark

adjusting knob

cable to control box

waterproof covering

search coil

The control box

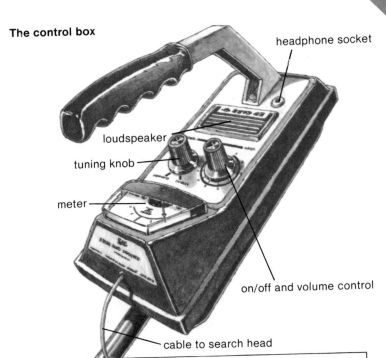

headphone socket

loudspeaker

tuning knob

meter

on/off and volume control

cable to search head

The search area

As long as you learn how to use your machine properly, it is not important to know exactly what goes on inside the search head and the control box. But you should realize that the search area below the head is roughly the shape shown on the right.

The most sensitive part, the area where the machine scans the earth most deeply, is directly under the centre of the search coil. You only have to miss a deep-lying coin by a few centimetres as you search and you will never know that it is there.

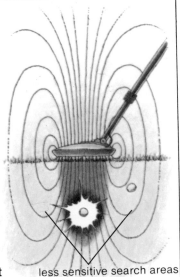

less sensitive search areas

15

Learning to use your detector

Using a detector is very exciting. But it is something that's easy to do badly and hard to do very well. You can prove this for yourself. The first place you search will probably be your own garden or that of a friend. Come back and try again in the same place after you have been using your detector for a month. You will find more targets there, however carefully you thought you were searching the first time, simply because you have become better at using the machine.

Practice makes perfect

At first you are bound to make mistakes, like going too fast or holding the search head too far above the ground. If you are going to get the most out of your detector, you must practise working slowly and carefully. An experienced searcher with a cheap machine will always find more than a beginner with a smart, expensive one. Practice is the key to success.

If you swing the detector to and fro like this, you will miss half the targets in your search area. The detector head is far too high at each end of the sweep.

Moving the head in a straight line like this is more difficult. But it makes sure that you really cover every inch of the ground and find everything buried there.

On beaches, in fields or on grass, mark out a lane 1.5 metres wide, using lolly sticks or large stones. This will help you keep track of the areas you still have to search.

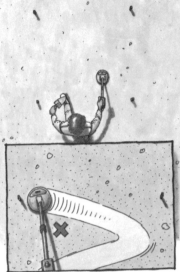

Search slowly and very thoroughly, moving the head in a straight line and overlapping slightly.

A fast, zig-zag search pattern can often take you straight past the best find of the day.

The 'lines and pins' method

Marking out lanes and working in straight lines may seem like a lot of trouble. But it is a method that makes sure that no important treasure has slipped through your fingers. When you sweep the detector head from side to side, try to make each sweep overlap with the one before. When you've done one lane, move the sticks from one side and place them the same distance away on the other side.

Archaeologists call this method the 'lines and pins' approach, because they tie a line of string between the pegs or lolly sticks they use to mark the lanes. On a large search site, it is often difficult to know where to start. If you do not have time to cover the whole area, walk briskly across it, swinging the detector in front of you, until you pick up one or two signals. Beginning your search here should bring good results. Come back later to search the rest of the site.

In the town

Many people think that the countryside is the best place to look for treasure. But there are more people in towns and therefore more finds to be made there. The single big hoard may well be lying in some farmer's field, but think how many other fields you might have to search before you found it. In the town you should be able to locate a steady stream of interesting and perhaps valuable finds.

Research

Success is mainly a matter of careful research. You will probably spend more time in your local library than actually walking around with your detector, but the results will be worth it. Some professional treasure hunters spend weeks finding out about the history of a site before they begin searching.

Every garden is worth searching.

Always get permission to search in parks.

Think of all the places in towns where people gather, out in the open, to enjoy themselves. Private gardens, parks and recreation grounds, sports fields and the small greens which form part of many modern housing estates are all worth searching. As long as you can convince the local council or whoever owns the land that you are not going to cause any damage, you should be able to find plenty of promising sites.

The right approach
Some people may need persuading before they let you loose on their gardens — and they will probably be sure that there is nothing there anyway. They are wrong. I have never found a single garden where even a quick search didn't turn up several coins and other items. Borrow a camera and take a series of pictures to show how neatly you dig up your finds. It will help you get permission to search all sorts of sites.

In the garden

Practise using your equipment in the garden.

If you are going to search for treasure with a metal detector, start at home, in your garden. Even while you are saving up for a detector, you can teach yourself how to dig up your finds properly. Learn to do it so neatly that you leave no mark at all, even on a smooth lawn. Grown-ups spend a lot of time on their gardens and the last thing they want to see is a ruined lawn. Show your parents how careful you are, so that they can help you persuade friends and neighbours to let you search their gardens too.

Where to begin

Back gardens produce more finds than front gardens, because people usually spend more time in them. In the front garden, search near the gate, along the sides of the path and around the front door. People fumbling for keys at night often drop coins. At the back, the whole garden should be searched, but pay special attention to the areas around old trees.

Searching on grass

1. Always use a small trowel. There is no need to use anything larger. Hold the trowel pointing straight down and make a neat cut in the turf, about 5cm to the side of where you think the target is. Then make two more cuts, as shown, so that you have marked out a rough horseshoe shape in the grass.

2. You should now be able to lift back a flap or 'cap' of turf, still attached to the rest of the lawn by the 'hinge' you have left at the back. This will allow you to replace the grass exactly as it was before. Often the target will be found embedded in the underside of the cap of turf, though it may be hidden by a plug of hard-packed soil.

3. Now dig down carefully, placing each trowel of earth on to a plastic carrier bag or polythene sheet beside the hole. If you cannot find the target, move the trowel out of the way and check the hole, the turf cap and the earth on the plastic sheet, by passing the head of the detector over them.

4. When you have found your target, pour the earth back into the hole. You will have to press it down a little, as there is always more earth to put back than the hole seems to need. Lift the flap back over the hole and tread it down firmly. If the grass is dry, sprinkle a little water over it.

Where to take your detector

Different search sites produce different types of treasure. If you want to find large numbers of fairly modern coins, you should search gardens, parks, commons, public footpaths or busy holiday beaches. But if you are determined to look for items that are a hundred years old or more, you must learn to recognise pointers to the past.

An old tree, or a stump, with a width of one metre or more will be at least two hundred years old. Oak trees can live for 500 years and yews for twice that time. A huge old tree that stands out as a landmark today will have been just as noticeable 100 years ago. Whenever you can, obtain permission to search around old buildings, trees and pathways.

Other ideas
Why not offer to find buried arrows on archery butts or recover lost property on camping sites, in return for permission to carry out a full search?

Searching for lost property on a camping site.

Do's and Don'ts

Deciding where to search with your metal detector is partly a question of choosing a promising site and partly a matter of getting permission to search there. Every bit of land belongs to somebody and you should always make sure you have **written permission** from the owner.

For searches on private land, including farm fields and gardens, you should write out an agreement between yourself and the landowner, which you should both sign. This should say that you both agree to share the value of any finds and that the landowner gives his permission for the search.

If you want to search parks or commons you will have to write to the **Parks Manager** of your council or local authority. Explain that you are interested in local history, that you would like to search for and recover coins and other items from the **top 15cms of the soil** and that you will cause no mess or damage.

If you have taken pictures to show how neatly you extract your finds, send him copies with your letter.

On public beaches, permission is not usually needed. If anyone questions you, just show them your detector licence.

Do wear gloves to protect your hands.
Do get permission in writing before you begin to search.
Do hand in all gold, silver and valuables to the police.
Do keep proper notes of all your finds.
Do report any historic finds to a museum.
Do leave search sites neat and tidy.

Don't go digging up official archaeological sites.
Don't search in old mines, quarries and caves. They are always disappointing and they can be dangerous.
Don't touch anything that could possibly be a shell or a bomb. Call in the police.
Don't dig so far into a dump that you leave a big overhang of earth. It could fall in and hurt you quite badly.

Coins, medals and badges

The earliest true coins were made in Turkey in about 600 BC. They were little blobs of electrum, a natural 'alloy' of gold and silver. Since then, most coins have been made of gold, silver, copper, bronze or modern copper and nickel alloys.

Try to arrange a visit to a museum with a good coin collection — you will soon see why numismatics, the study of coins, is one of the world's most popular hobbies.

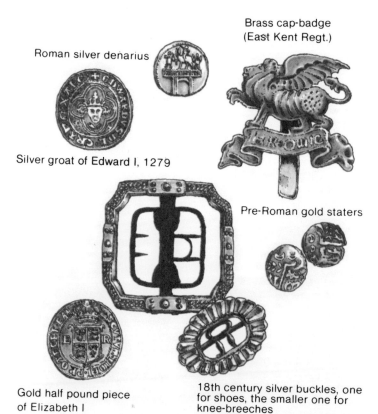

Roman silver denarius

Brass cap-badge
(East Kent Regt.)

Silver groat of Edward I, 1279

Pre-Roman gold staters

Gold half pound piece
of Elizabeth I

18th century silver buckles, one
for shoes, the smaller one for
knee-breeches

World War I medal
(1914-15 Star)

Spanish-American silver cobs.
the famous Pieces of Eight

Austrian thaler, 1632

Massachusetts
Oak Tree shilling

George III halfcrown, 1818

Cap-badge of the
Sherwood Foresters

Edward VII sovereign

Copper penny, 1860

Australian florin, 1945

Modern British 50 pence piece

1908 US $20 gold piece

Rivers and canals

Rivers and streams are important treasure hunting sites. In ancient times, towns grew up around places where a river was shallow enough to wade or ride across, or where it was narrow enough for a bridge to be built or a ferryboat to make regular crossings. Everyone entering or leaving the town would do so by these few bridges, ferries and fords, and armies in retreat would also seek a river crossing — otherwise they would find themselves trapped.

Even 200 years ago, in the days before railways and proper roads, a river or canal barge was much the best way of moving heavy loads around the country.

For all these reasons, huge numbers of coins, weapons, bottles and clay pipes have been dropped into or near rivers and canals over the centuries.

Where to look

Just searching on the banks often produces good finds, particularly if you rake or sieve the mud in areas that look especially promising. With a metal detector you stand an even better chance of finding things. Search towpaths and the approaches to bridges and fords. But remember, water can be dangerous — so put safety first and don't take any risks.

Mudding

The mud and sand of an estuary or foreshore is an excellent place to search — but make sure that it is absolutely safe. Take a plastic sieve with you, as wet mud can sometimes give confusing false signals. Try putting a few spadefuls of mud in your sieve, lifting it several centimetres clear of the ground and scanning across it with your detector. If there is a target hidden in the mud you will now hear a good, clear signal.

River finds can be very old. The Roman soldiers or merchants for example, would never cross a river without tossing in a coin as a gift to please their gods.

Sieving the river gravel

In the country

If you approach a farmer in the middle of summer and ask for permission to look for bottle dumps or search his fields with a detector, the answer will almost certainly be 'no'. In the autumn when crops have been harvested, or during the winter and early spring, he is much more likely to agree.

Searching ploughed fields

People used to think that the older a coin was, the deeper it would have sunk in the soil. But many hoards and very old single coins have been found with cheap BFO metal detectors, simply because both ploughing and the action of earthworms are constantly turning the topsoil over.

Other good sites
The list is almost endless: roadside verges, village greens, woods, commons and the banks of ponds and streams all yield fascinating finds. Search fairground sites and market places, picnic areas and steep slopes that are used as sledge runs in winter.

Look out for clues
Learn to recognize landmarks that have remained unchanged for hundreds of years, such as crossroads, winding country lanes and footpaths, old trees, milestones, and wind and water mills.

Many hedgerows are also very old and you can work out their age by pacing out a 30 metre stretch and counting the different types of shrub and tree in that section. The number of types of plant will be roughly the number of centuries the hedge has been there.

On the beach

Beaches are always good places to look for treasure. The action of the sea slowly brings ashore bits of wreckage, old coins, bottles and cannon balls from the thousands of ships which have been sunk by storms or lost in battle near our coasts. You may not be lucky enough to find a handful of Pieces of Eight from a Spanish galleon or the ship's wheel from a sunken merchantman, but such finds do turn up on beaches year after year.

Searching the tideline

The best time to search for this kind of treasure is after a storm. Walk along the high tide line, but keep a sharp lookout in the area just below it as well. When there have been no storms or very high tides in the last few days, you will see two distinct tide lines. Check both of them thoroughly, and the strip of sand or shingle between them.

Finds washed ashore by the sea

▲ A 'glory hole' is a place where the current has deposited a cluster of coins. Scan any patches of coin-sized pebbles and dig down if you start to find coins – it could be your lucky day!

▲ Objects are carried along by waves breaking at an angle. Search around groynes. Coins may be trapped on the windward side or swept round to lie in the piled-up sand downwind.

Coinshooting

If you have a metal detector, you will find that popular holiday beaches are ideal sites for coinshooting as millions of coins, watches and rings are lost there every summer.

Take your detector to the beach in the evening, after the crowds have left. Search the tide line first and then concentrate on the areas where people sit — in the shelter of a groyne or sea wall, near steps down to the beach, near piles of deck-chairs and around refreshment kiosks.

What to do with your finds

Always collect any silver paper or ring-pulls from drink cans and dispose of them in a litter bin. Otherwise you may waste time digging up the same rubbish the next day. Remember to hand in all watches, rings and purses to the police. They will be returned to you if they are not claimed.

Bottle dumps

Digging your way through a hundred year old rubbish dump does not sound as exciting as using a metal detector. Your treasure will be made up of bottles, stone ginger beer jars and the china lids from old pots of shaving cream and toothpaste, rather than gold or silver coins. But if you can pinpoint a single dump which has not already been dug, you may find yourself digging up hundreds of beautiful bottles and potlids.

Why dig for bottles?

Bottles come in a fascinating variety of shapes and many brilliant colours. Keen collectors in Britain, America, South Africa and Australia pay very high prices for rare specimens.

With a metal detector, there is always a chance of finding a hoard of ancient coins. But there are a lot more undiscovered bottle dumps around than there are pots of gold pieces.

Most of the rubbish thrown away on Victorian dumps has long since rotted into the soil – leaving bottles which can be worth a small fortune.

Historic rubbish

A hundred years ago, there were no dustmen, except in the main towns. In the country, the only way to get rid of rubbish was to dig a pit a little way from the house (and preferably downwind of it) and dump it there. Every house of any size had its own dump. There was no tinned or frozen food and almost everything, from boot polish and hair grease to meat extract, was sold in bottles or pots.

Each family must have thrown away hundreds of these every year, so it is no exaggeration to say that even a small private dump could yield a thousand or more bottles.

Major sites

In large towns, there was already an organized rubbish collection service. The waste was taken in carts to tips outside the town or loaded onto barges and taken several miles away. If you locate one of these big dumps, it could keep you busy for months on end.

Tell-tale signs of an old bottle dump are large clumps of nettles and bits of china and broken bottles littering the surface.

Nettles grow best where the soil is very rich in nitrogen and phosphates, both of which are formed as rubbish rots away.

The beauty of bottles

A good collection of bottles and stoneware can be incredibly beautiful. The range of shapes, colours and sizes — from delicate ink bottles to sturdy pop and beer bottles — is much greater than most people realize. Two of the most famous collector's items are the chunky torpedo-shaped Hamilton and the Codd, which had a marble trapped in the neck as a stopper. They were both used for fizzy drinks.

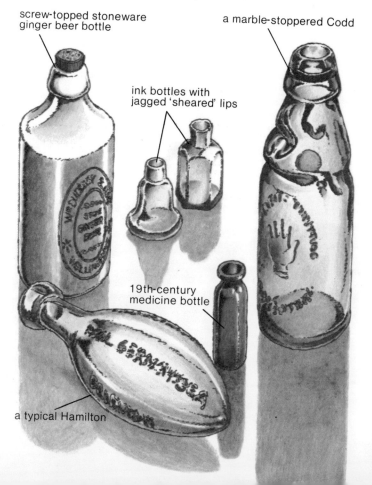

screw-topped stoneware
ginger beer bottle

a marble-stoppered Codd

ink bottles with
jagged 'sheared' lips

19th-century
medicine bottle

a typical Hamilton

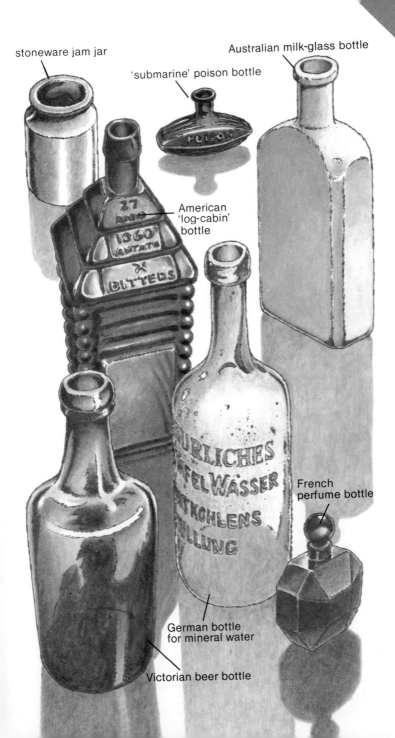

stoneware jam jar

'submarine' poison bottle

Australian milk-glass bottle

POISON

American 'log-cabin' bottle

37
1860
BITTERS

...ÜRLICHES
...FFELWASSER
...NTKOHLENS
...ÜLLUNG

French perfume bottle

German bottle for mineral water

Victorian beer bottle

Cleaning up your finds

Cleaning the inside with gravel and water.

When to start cleaning
Never clean bottles for at least a day after you dig them up. When they are buried, stresses and strains are set up in the glass, because of the damp and the weight of earth pressing down on them. Glass is actually a very slow-moving liquid and your bottles will soon readjust to the release of pressure. But if you try to clean them straightaway, they will probably shatter.

Outside dirt
This can often be loosened by thrusting the bottle into a bucket of soft sand and twisting it in different directions. The sand scours the glass clean.

Cleaning inside
Soak the bottle in lukewarm water and then use a small bottle brush. You can make one by cutting a strip from a spiky nylon hair roller and fixing it to a piece of cane. If there are corners that still will not come clean, put some gravel in the bottle and fill it halfway with water. Place your thumb over the end and shake vigorously.

Stains
Remove stains by rubbing with lemon juice or vinegar and then rinsing thoroughly. Badly stained bottles should be soaked for at least 48 hours, in a bucket of water with half a kilo of washing soda dissolved in it.

How to clean coins

Cleaning old coins is a job that should really be left to the experts. Coins can easily be scratched and damaged and a badly cleaned coin will lose much of its value. Many dealers have a strict rule against buying coins, however old and rare, which have already been cleaned up by amateur collectors.

Gold coins are often dug up in surprisingly good condition, because gold is not 'corroded' (eaten away) by air, water or chemicals in the soil.

Very dirty **gold** and **silver** coins can be gently washed with soap and water. Do not rub or scrub them, as this will produce hundreds of tiny scratches which ruin the surface of the coin.

Old **copper** coins can be cleaned with a soft brush, but must never be washed.

Modern coins

Most of the coins you find will be modern. The best thing to do with them is to clean them up, any way you like, and then go out and spend them – or save them up towards the cost of a better metal detector.

Coins which are old enough or odd enough to be interesting items in your collection can be cleaned in a number of ways – but do remember not to use them on your really important finds. These methods make coins look shiny, but can destroy their value.

Coppers can be placed in Worcester sauce for an hour, or dipped for five minutes in a mixture of white vinegar and salt and then rinsed thoroughly.

Silver coins can be rubbed gently with a paste made from baking soda and a few drops of water.

Ultrasonic cleaners
If you want to take cleaning seriously, it is now possible to buy a small ultrasonic cleaning device, like the one on the left, for about £12.

This is similar to the units used in museums for cleaning metal artefacts. It is far less likely to damage your finds than the electrolytic coin cleaners sold in some shops, which can cause pitting on the surface of the coin.

Where to look for coins

Lost coins, rings and other valuables do not stay
exactly where they are dropped. They sink in the soil,
are moved around by the action of earthworms and are
brought to the surface or pushed down even deeper as
farmers plough the land.

Some of these movements cannot be predicted, but
many of them can. On beaches, the most sensational
finds usually occur after big storms have churned up
the sand. Inland, the forces that re-shape the
landscape are less spectacular and violent. But they are
going on all the time.

River bends
Rivers and streams always carry mud and stones (and
coins) downstream. These will be deposited where the
water slows down, on the inside of a bend.

In the picture below, valuables dropped from the old
bridge centuries before will eventually work their way
down to the part of the bank where the treasure hunter
is searching.

This boy knows just where to look.

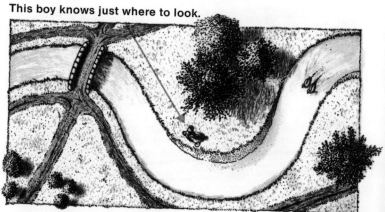

Trees

Tree stumps and old trees, especially any with trunks a metre or more across, are clues to important search areas. Check any holes around the roots and hollows in the trunk for hoards and then work carefully outwards with the detector. If there is a mat of dead leaves below the tree, older coins will probably have sunk out of detector range. But the network of roots may have caught some of them and stopped them sinking too far.

Paths

Footpaths are key search areas, but remember that when they are wet and muddy, people usually walk at the sides of the path. So search both sides, as well as on the path itself. If the path or track is on a hillside, search slightly further down the slope. The slow slipping movement of the soil itself can carry your targets several metres downhill from the path.

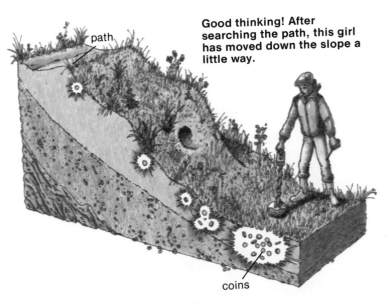

path

Good thinking! After searching the path, this girl has moved down the slope a little way.

coins

Keeping records

Using a notebook
It is very important to write down details of all your finds. You might, for example, visit a new site and make some interesting discoveries but then be unable to return there for a couple of weeks. When you do make another visit, your notebook will remind you of which areas you have already searched, of what you found and exactly where you discovered it. Every good site is always worth at least two visits.

A sketch map
Make a rough sketch map of your site and mark the position of each find on it as you go along. This can help you to notice a pattern – such as all your finds being more or less in line. It could mean that you have discovered a forgotten footpath. Following the line could produce good results.

Keep all your notebooks and give each one a number, so that you can refer back from your index cards to your field notes.

A typical notebook page

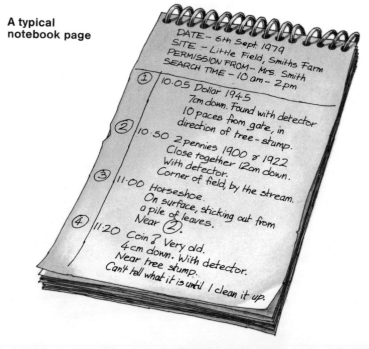

DATE – 6th Sept. 1979
SITE – Little Field, Smiths Farm
PERMISSION FROM – Mrs. Smith
SEARCH TIME – 10 am – 2 pm

① 10.05 Dollar 1945
7cm down. Found with detector
10 paces from gate, in direction of tree-stump.

② 10.50 2 pennies 1900 & 1922
Close together 12cm down.
With detector.
Corner of field, by the stream.

③ 11.00 Horseshoe.
On surface, sticking out from a pile of leaves.
Near ②.

④ 11.20 Coin? Very old.
4cm down. With detector.
Near tree stump.
Can't tell what it is until I clean it up.

A card index file

This is the best way to record the details of all your interesting finds. It allows you to check up the facts about them at a moment's notice.

Keep two separate index files, one for bottles and dump finds and the other for coins.

Bottles

Make out a card for each bottle, with the size in centimetres at the top and a coloured dot in the top right-hand corner. Try to match the colour of the dot to the colour of the glass. Draw a small circle for clear glass bottles, and use squares, rather than dots, for ginger beer bottles and stoneware.

Arranging the cards

Place them in order of size, so that you can find the card for, say, a 12cm green bottle, in a matter of seconds. On each card write a description of your find, say when and where you found it and add the number of the notebook containing that day's field notes.

Coins

Arrange your coin card index in date order, with dots of yellow, grey or brown for gold, silver and copper coins. Write down everything you can find out about each coin, and say when and where you found it. Add how deeply each one was buried and the number of that day's notebook.

Hoards

Searching for hoards is the most exciting kind of treasure hunting. Each year, several hundred people turn up hoards valued at a thousand pounds or more. Until a few years ago, most large hoards were found by accident, by farmworkers, builders or demolition workers who were just doing their normal jobs. But these days more and more hoards are being found by treasure hunters who know what they are looking for.

Second time lucky
The best place to look for a hoard is where one has already been found. In the old days, wealthy people did not want to put all their eggs in one basket: a man who wanted to hide his treasure safely would often divide it up into two or three parts and bury them separately. It is worth spending some time looking through local history books and old newspapers to find out where hoards have been found in your area.

They can turn up in the most remote and unlikely places — because it is safer for people to bury their wealth in a deserted spot than somewhere where they might be seen.

Using your imagination

Imagine that you are a rich medieval merchant, on your way from one market to the next. It is evening and you come over the brow of a hill and see a town ahead of you. Will the people be friendly? Or will they rob you of everything you have? You decide to hide your gold and go down into the town to look around. What could be more sensible? But suppose you are attacked and murdered, or fall ill and die in that strange town. Your money is safe, but you cannot go back to collect it and it may be hundreds of years before some boy or girl with a detector hears an odd bleep from the machine and finds your forgotten treasure.

Some big finds

Sensational finds turn up year after year, all over the world. Some of them were hidden by rich people worried about wars or the plague. Others were hastily buried, or even thrown off bridges into rivers, by robbers on the run, who were desperate to hide their loot.

The hoards on these two pages were all found in the last few years, either by treasure hunters carrying out special searches or by people who just happened to stumble across them. But remember, although most of these hoards look very spectacular, a single very rare coin in good condition can be worth thousands of pounds to collectors.

Bandit gold! This hoard was found by an American treasure hunter on holiday in Mexico.

French treasure; a pitcher full of coins and jewellery, found in the wall of an old building.

This gold piece turned up on an old racecourse. It is worth $300,000.

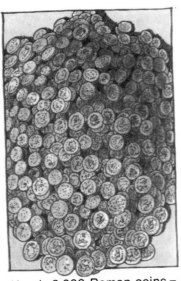

Nearly 3,000 Roman coins – they were located in a field on an English farm.

Two English 15-year-olds found these 97 gold coins in a wood. The hoard was valued at £25,000.

With the help of a metal detector, this large nugget was found in the Australian goldfields.

Clues from the past

Whether you are searching for buried hoards, bottle dumps or good sites for 'coinshooting' expeditions, research will always help. Studying the history and geography of your area, looking at old maps and newspapers and reading the oldest books you can find about your town or village should become an important part of your treasure hunting plan. Your history teacher and the local librarian can both help you find the clues you need. Luck becomes less and less important as you begin to build up your own file of notes about the history of local sites.

The Black Death
The more history you know, the more you will understand about how people used to live and where and why they might have lost or hidden their valuables. For example, when the plague, the Black Death, swept across Europe in the 14th century, people fled in terror from their homes. With no reliable banks to look after their wealth, many of them 'banked' their money in the ground.

Wars and riots

Rioting and wars, especially civil wars, caused the same sort of panic as the plague. Whenever people were frightened or worried, they would hide their valuables. So it is not really surprising that the value of buried treasure found every year adds up to millions of pounds.

Talking to old people

Read everything you can find about the history of your area, but don't forget that you can pick up valuable clues by talking to people who have lived there for many years. Talk to old people about the stories and customs they remember from their childhood. Ask them about markets and fairs and where the rubbish used to be dumped.

Ask your grandparents to tell you the stories they heard from their parents and grandparents. Your grandfather's grandfather could well have been born before the battle of Waterloo, before the railways were invented and before Queen Victoria was born!

Old people can be a mine of information.

How old is it?

Dating the bottles, potlids and pipes that you have found can be difficult. The simplest way to do it is to find all the clues you can and then make a guess at the age of the whole dump. All the finds from one dump will usually date from the same period.

The tell-tale seam

Look first at the bottles. Examine the seam that runs up the side of a bottle, the mark left by the glass-blower's mould. If it runs right up to and through the lip at the very top, the bottle was made by machine.

This is a useful guide to the age of the dump, as automatic bottle-making machines were not invented until 1887.

Clay pipes

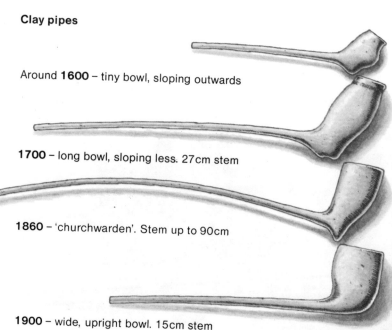

Around **1600** – tiny bowl, sloping outwards

1700 – long bowl, sloping less. 27cm stem

1860 – 'churchwarden'. Stem up to 90cm

1900 – wide, upright bowl. 15cm stem

Pipes, stoneware and potlids

Clay pipes were very popular for over 300 years, right up to the end of the 19th century. About that time, people began to prefer cigarettes to pipes. So a dump with many broken clay pipes is almost always at least 70 years old. Stone ginger beer bottles started having printed transfer patterns and writing in about 1890, while black and white — and later coloured — potlid designs were popular from the early 19th century until about 1910.

Rich colours mean good finds

If you keep finding bottles made of clear glass, or bits of plastic, your dump is probably too modern to be very exciting. But if there are plenty of coloured bottles, with air bubbles in the glass and perhaps embossed writing on the sides, it is very likely to be a good late-19th century site.

Bottles

Beer bottles from (left to right) 1700, 1825, 1870, 1900 and the present day. The early bottles had loose-fitting wedge-shaped corks tied on with string. The invention of corkscrews, which happened around 1720, made it possible to use tight-fitting corks for the first time. This meant that bottles could be stored on their sides and led to the development of the familiar cylindrical shape. Then came heavy screw stoppers and finally today's metal crown caps.

Archaeological sites

As your treasure hunting experience builds up, you will find your interest in history growing. You may decide to join your local historical or archaeological society. But many dump-diggers and metal detector users have found that historians and archaeologists do not understand their hobbies.

Protected sites

The problem is that a few stupid people have given metal detectors a bad name by sneaking on to archaeological sites and causing terrible damage. These 'pirates' are breaking the law, as it is illegal to interfere with protected sites. They do not care that they may be ruining important evidence about our past as they are only interested in finding valuable objects, and they do not hand in their finds to the police or inform museum staff of important discoveries. They are not true treasure hunters.

Archaeologists sometimes claim too that digging up detector finds on any site destroys the **'stratification'** (the pattern of layers in the soil) and should be banned.

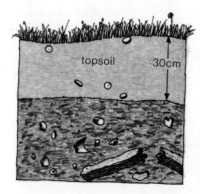

topsoil   30cm

Ploughing, garden digging and the constant movement of worms all churn up the soil to a depth of at least 30cm. The topsoil is never 'stratified' at this sort of depth – and only a few, extremely expensive, professional detectors can go any deeper. The stratified layers containing archeological evidence begin below this covering of topsoil.

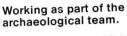
Working as part of the archaeological team.

No sensible treasure hunter with an inexpensive detector will be digging down deep enough to spoil the stratification — except perhaps in a very few places where the topsoil is extremely shallow. These treasure hunters agree with the archaeologists that the 'pirates' must be stopped. Otherwise their behaviour could lead to calls for a ban on the use of metal detectors.

Helping the archaeologists

Individuals and clubs can sometimes use their metal detectors to help on official archaeological sites. There have been several successful projects recently where treasure hunters have agreed to work under the guidance of teams of archaeologists. Why not contact your local museum or historical society and offer to help out on an official 'dig'?

Tools and weapons

Although you are hoping to find coins or bottles, never throw away the other objects you unearth until you are quite sure they are junk. The Bronze Age sword hilt (bottom left) is over 3,000 years old, but when it was dug up, covered in dirt, no-one realised at first what an important find it was. Tools, weapons and smaller items like keys, cutlery and musket balls can form an interesting part of your collection.

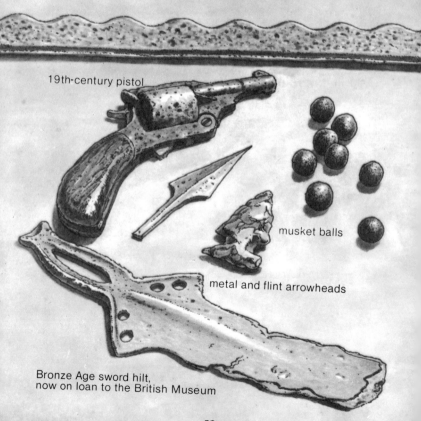

19th-century pistol

musket balls

metal and flint arrowheads

Bronze Age sword hilt, now on loan to the British Museum

52

horseshoe and nails

ceremonial sword

spearhead

18th-century knife

a selection of old keys

pistol and
rifle bullets

Displaying your finds

Coin albums

Coin collectors usually keep their coins in albums or in beautifully made coin cabinets with locking doors and dozens of shallow drawers about 2cm deep. But cabinets are very expensive pieces of furniture. Albums are cheap. Each page has rows of small clear plastic envelopes to put the coins in.

Albums like this are very useful for holding common coins and modern issues, but a rare and special coin really deserves something a little better.

A display card

Make a neat pocket for each coin by cutting a strip of cellophane slightly wider than the coin and just over twice as long. Fold the cellophane in half, stick the edges together at either side with clear sticky tape and attach the pocket to a large piece of card. Stick a label underneath with details of each coin and how you found it.

Why not try grouping, say, all your silver coins or all your Roman finds together, so that each card has a special theme?

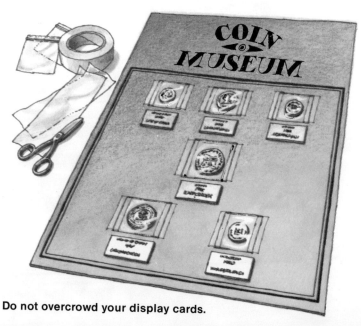

Do not overcrowd your display cards.

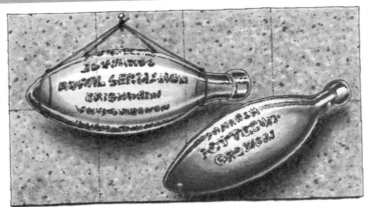

▲ After cleaning, bottles can be given a superb shine by polishing with cerium oxide. This is a red powder that you can buy from a jeweller or a craft shop. If you cannot find any, rub your bottles with a few drops of light machine oil. This gives a good shine, but it only lasts a few weeks before the bottles need washing again. Hamiltons are difficult to display properly, but you can hang them as shown above, using a cradle of string or supporting each bottle with a large cuphook and a nail.

▲Coloured glass really comes to life when you can see the light shining through it. Some bottle collectors build complicated display units with special lighting to show off their best finds. But you can get the same effect much more easily by building a window shelf. This can be as simple as a plank of wood, supported at each end by a pair of bricks on the window sill. Choose just a few of your most interesting bottles — do not be tempted to crowd your shelf. Blue, aqua green and light brown all look terrific in strong sunlight.

Be a treasure hunter —

and not a pirate!

Treasure hunting is perhaps the wrong name for this fascinating and enjoyable pastime. But the name has stuck as the hobby has grown during the past ten years or so. It reminds people of hair-raising tales of wicked pirates with a terrible greed for gold. We have our own pirates of course — the vandals who damage and steal from archaeological sites. But they are getting fewer and fewer as they are caught and punished.

The fun of searching
For most treasure hunters, the hobby is concerned with the enjoyment of finding objects which have not been touched by human hands for tens or even hundreds of years.

Occasionally, a keen treasure hunter may stumble upon a hoard which could make him rich overnight. But even then he often cannot bear to part with his treasure. It is worth far more than money to him.

The positive side

Treasure hunting is more than simply searching with a detector or digging up dumps. Keen treasure hunters build up fine collections of coins, bottles and other objects of interest. Their grasp of history and geography grows as they make the mental leap into the past to try to understand how people used to live. History lessons at school suddenly come to life. Parents too, find that treasure hunting is a hobby that the whole family can enjoy.

People who are against metal detectors see only the bad side: the damage caused by the pirates. But real treasure hunters are finding new sites for the archaeologists to work on and are helping to fill gaps in the jigsaw of history by finding ancient coins, tools and weapons which were previously unknown.

Reference section
Treasure hunters and the law

Treasure hunters in the United States are very lucky. In many countries, the law is very strict about where you can search. Here, as long as you can obtain permission from the landowner and avoid restricted areas, you are allowed to search almost anywhere.

If you do find a hoard of gold or silver, while the U.S. and state governments have a claim to buried treasure in certain circumstances, you can be sure you will either be allowed to keep most of it, and in some cases, all of it; or be paid a very fair reward for your discovery.

State laws

Most treasure finds must be reported to the authorities in the state in which they are found. Every state has laws governing the discovery of treasure.

This can also hold true when treasure is discovered under the waters off the shore of a particular state rather than under the ground. For example, the state of Florida has laws that say it owns all treasure discovered in waters from the shore to three miles out and the state will retain one quarter of the value of whatever is found in the Atlantic Ocean or the Gulf of Mexico.

The waters off the coast of Florida are particularly rich in sunken treasure because of the many gold and jewel laden Spanish galleons that went down in those areas in the 18th century. By no means have all of these treasure ships been recovered.

An information packet on the laws governing treasure hunting in Florida's waters can be obtained by writing to
Department of State
Division of Archives and History
Underwater Research Section
The Capitol
Tallahassee, FL 32304

Every state library, located in the state capital, will have information on the laws governing treasure searches and finds within the state. An excellent source of information may be the library or museum nearest to the site in which you are interested.

Writing to the Superintendent of Documents, U.S. Government Printing Office, Washington, DC 20402, can also help you with your treasure hunting. There are many government publications on searching for gold and other treasures.

Prospecting

Prospecting is a particularly American form of treasure hunting. One of the most famous treasure stories of the Southwest revolves around the Lost Dutchman Mine, supposedly located in the Superstition Mountains of Arizona. This mysterious gold mine, "discovered" and lost again several times in the 19th and early 20th centuries, still lures treasure hunters to comb the mountains of the area in the hope of once more finding a great golden treasure.

Other modern-day treasure hunters pan for gold in the streams of the ore-bearing areas of California, Nevada, and Alaska. There have been many reported finds of gold dust, gold flakes, and even some nuggets.

If you are interested in prospecting, the U.S. Department of the Interior's Bureau of Mines will supply you with information and direct you to spots where earth formations indicate gold may be found.

Scuba diving

The use of self-contained underwater breathing apparatus for diving, is known as scuba diving. Scuba diving has changed the whole field of treasure hunting at sea. Most of the Spanish galleons that were known to have sunk as they sailed between the new and old worlds, went down off the coast of the southeastern United States.

While their general locations and cargos are roughly known from old records, it takes skilled scuba divers to search the waters and find the ships that have been buried beneath shifting sands for hundreds of years.

Anyone who can swim can learn scuba diving. Most areas, and especially those in coastal states, have schools that teach scuba diving and usually shops that sell the specialized equipment for underwater treasure hunting. The Yellow Pages of your phone directory will probably be the most direct way of finding them.

Museums

Often your local museums will have a file on treasures that have been found right in your area and they will gladly share their knowledge with you.

However, for those particularly interested in treasure from the sea, there are museums that have specialized in displaying treasures recovered from the ocean. Writing them will bring much information. Their names and addresses are listed below:

Chicago Historical Society
Clark St. at North Ave.
Chicago, IL 60614

Florida State Museum
The Capitol
Tallahassee, FL 32304

New Orleans Museum of Art
(A) Lelong Avenue
City Park
P.O. Box 19123
New Orleans, LA 70179

The Smithsonian Institution
1000 Jefferson Drive, SW
Washington, DC 20560

Clubs and associations

For the beginner, joining a treasure hunting club is a very good way to get started. You will meet other interested people, some of them with years of experience in metal detecting and bottle dump digging. Club visits to tried and tested sites will help you over the problem of getting permission for private searches, give you the chance to practice, and probably lead to some interesting finds.

If you would like to work on protected sites alongside professional archeologists, this can be arranged much more easily through a club, or through your school, rather than on your own. Most colleges and universities often have some type of "dig" going on, and perhaps arrangements can be made for you to join it. Many schools have formed their own clubs, often under the direction of a history or geography teacher.

One word of warning, however, must be said to all treasure hunters — don't buy any so-called treasure maps, no matter what you are told. The only maps worth using are those the United States government will sell you that outline the mineral possibilities in your area. Any others merely represent wishful dreaming, and the mapmaker is the one who will find the fortune — right in your pocket!

Here is a list of several organizations to whom you might want to write.

Associated Geographers of America,
P.O. Box 188,
Midway City, CA 92655

Circle of Companions,
One Examino Building,
Segundo, CO 81070

National Treasure Hunters League,
1309 W. 21st St.
Tempe, AZ 85282

Prospectors Club Intl.
P.O. Box 2081,
Indianapolis, IN 46206

Prospector's and Treasure Hunters Guild,
Segundo, CO 81070

Booklist

If you have enjoyed this book, you will probably want to find out more about treasure hunting and bottle collecting.

There are only a handful of good books on the subject and it is probably best to borrow them from the library before you decide whether to buy them or not.

Treasure and Treasure Hunters ed. by R. Armstrong (David White Company)

Treasure Galleons by D.L. Harner (Dodd, Mead & Co.)

Treasure Hunter's Guide by E. Fletcher, (Sterling Publishing)

Treasure Hunter's Manual, No. 7 by K. Von Muller, (Ram Publishing Co.)

Treasure Hunting in the USA by N. Carlisle (Popular Library)

Treasure Hunting Manual (International Publications)

Bottles by R. Stewart and G. Caentino (Western Publishing)

Bottles, Value and Identification Guide ed. by D. and C. Sellari (Wallace-Homestead)

Bottles, Yesterday's Trash, Today's Treasure by D. E. Calcleaser (Time Bottle Publishing Co.)

Magazines
Treasure (monthly), *Treasure Hunting Unlimited* (quarterly), and *Treasure Search* (Bi-monthly).

Glossary

Alloy: a metal made by mixing two or more other metals together.

BFO detector: simplest, cheapest type of metal detector. Can be very good, if used with skill.

Cerium oxide: fine reddish powder. Mixed to a paste with a few drops of water for polishing glass.

Churchwarden: 19th-century clay pipe with a very long curved stem.

Codd: curious type of pop bottle, with a nipped-in neck and marble stopper.·

Coinshooting: searching with a detector for single coins.

Crown cap: modern metal bottle top with pinched-in sides to hold it on.

Denarius: Roman silver penny. In Britain's old £.s.d. coinage, the 'd' stood for denarius.

Embossing: raised writing or pattern on glass.

Glory hole: a particular spot where many coins are found close together.

Groat: English four penny piece, first issued in 1279.

Hamilton: bottle with a rounded base, so that it had to be laid on its side.

Hoard: a large quantity of buried treasure.

IB detector: medium-priced detector, sometimes more sensitive than a BFO.

Lines and pins search: slow, methodical way of searching a site thoroughly.

Milk glass: cloudy, pearl-like glass, white or coloured.

Mudding: searching for lost items in the mud of a river.

Pieces of Eight (cobs): rough silver coins, made by cutting slices off a silver bar and stamping a pattern on them.

Protected sites: ancient monuments, protected by law.

Stater: coin, like a gold blazer button, in use from pre-Roman times until 61 A.D.

Thaler (pronounced 'tarla'): large silver coin, originally made in Austria.

Ultrasonic cleaner: device to clean objects, using sound vibrations too high to be heard by the human ear.

Index